THE FIGHTER WORE
A SKIRT

Thirty-Two Gifted American Women
Who Faced a Challenge and Won

by Nancy Polette

Pieces of Learning

©2002 Nancy Polette
2002 First published
by Pieces of Learning
www.piecesoflearning.com
CLC0277
ISBN 1-931334-12-9
Printed in U.S.A.
Illustrated by Paul Dillon

Dedicated to
Sarah, Kate, Victoria, and Kaeleigh

THE FIGHTER WORE A SKIRT

Contents

THE FIGHTER WORE A SKIRT
Introduction

From 1775 to the present women have been fighters for many different freedoms. Molly Pitcher took her husband's place in battle. Dolley Madison saved White House treasures that are so much a part of the nation's legacy. Mary Harris Jones and Delores Huerta fought for workers' rights. Elizabeth Blackwell challenged the medical establishment for a woman's right to become a physician. Mary Colter wrestled the Grand Canyon. Bessie Coleman conquered the sky. Mary Lou Retton and Betty Schwartz overcame serious injuries to win the Olympic Gold. Mary Cassatt and Mary Kay Ash conquered the male-dominated fields of art and corporate finance. Thousands of babies are born healthy today because Frances Kelsey fought the drug companies.

The 32 narrative poems tell the struggles and accomplishments of these and other courageous women who were willing to fight for what they believed. Each had a passion that she was not afraid to pursue, although many lived at a time when women had little control over money, they frowned upon education for women, and the restrictions of society made it difficult to exercise freedom of action. Despite these and other difficulties, each woman excelled in her chosen field or cause. No study of American history is complete without their stories.

Note some birth and death dates are uncertain. Sources differ, for instance, about Calamity Jane's and Bessie Coleman's birth dates. Primary sources were used when possible.

FIRING THE CANNON

Mary Ludwig Hays McCauly (Molly Pitcher)
1753 - 1832
She fought beside the troops in the Revolutionary War

There she was
young, strong, determined
to stand with pride at her husband's side
to join him in the Revolution.
Washington's army needed men.
Molly's husband needed her.
Where he goes, she goes.
Told friends goodbye and packed her pots
to cook for him and wash his clothes.
The smell of gunpowder filled the air,
bullets whizzing everywhere.
Molly went from man to man
comforting the wounded without fear,
heeding the cries of
"Molly, Molly, over here!"
It was then she saw her husband fall.
Molly darted forward, hands reaching,
back straining she picked up the ramrod
and loaded the deadly cannonball.
Arms tired, she fired
again and again until the battle's end.

RUNNING BEFORE THE ENEMY

Elizabeth (Betty) Zane
1766 - 1831
A frontier heroine who saved Fort Henry

Elizabeth (Betty) Zane was daring
At seventeen she had a caring heart.
Fleet of foot
she ran with speed,
she sewed and cooked, learned how to read.
Other things that she could do:
preparing flax
weaving, too.
She won at games
and truth to tell
she did most everything quite well.

Returned from school to find a crowd
of frightened folk,
heads all bowed in prayer.
Gathered in the center court
of the military fort
searching for a way to halt
the deadly enemy's assault.
The attack grew louder
and still louder
Return the fire? No gun powder!

2

Without an adequate supply
of powder
men were sure to die.
The stores were at
her brother's house.
Betty, playing cat and mouse,
was fleet of foot
and ran unfazed.
The enemy watching,
stood amazed.

When the watchers
had no doubt
of what her mission was about,
they fired.
The bullets
pierced her clothes.
Not hit,
the girl escaped her foes.

The story of her escapade
to save the fort
is one of courage
well displayed.
With loaded guns
the men all strived
to fight until
relief arrived,
thanks to the efforts of a single maid
who breeched
the enemy's barricade.

PRESERVING A LEGACY

Dolley Madison
1768 - 1849
With the enemy at the door she rescued
White House treasures

She walks the empty rooms alone.
The guards have gone and so have friends.
The carriage, packed with cabinet papers,
awaits its passenger, but she delays again.

French John, a faithful servant
urges her to flee. She is hesitant.
"Not yet," she says, pointing to the wall,
"Take down the portrait of the President."

The artillery sounds grow louder.
Two messengers arrive and urge her to flee.
She rips the portrait from its frame.
"Take it," she shouts, "and follow me."

She takes the carriage reins,
with the loaded wagon behind,
leaving the British plunderers
with nothing of value to find.

That night the Capitol is torched,
Departments of War, Treasury and State,
The White House, too, but not its treasures,
The enemy had arrived too late.

CHEATING THE GUILLOTINE

Elizabeth Monroe 1768 - 1830
Rescuing a Woman from the Guillotine

"A lovely girl," people said
with dark eyes and impish grin,
but her family feared when
their fortune disappeared,
a life of genteel poverty.

A young girl who was praised
for her great beauty,
a New York City resident who
would marry a future president,
the serious and sober Monroe.

In 1794 she traveled across the sea
with her husband to France.
There, as the U.S. Minister, he would
discover a sinister plot
to behead the wife of Lafayette.

Head high, determined,
Elizabeth went to the prison
to ask authorities how they dare
behead the unfortunate woman there
and her efforts met with success.

In 1817 she became the First Lady
of the United States of America.
She was a woman of charm and grace
who had found the perfect place
to serve her country well.

EXPOSING THE HORRORS OF SLAVERY

Harriet Beecher Stowe
1811 - 1896
Author of *Uncle Tom's Cabin*, "The spark that started the war"

Look at her,
nose in a book
motherless child at the age of four
busily writing verses for
her father's sermons.

The young girl at thirteen
brilliant and bookish
following the Golden Rule
teaching in her sister's school
exciting young minds.

At age twenty-five
the bride of Calvin Stowe,
a clergyman in a small town,
a tiny vision in her wedding gown,
a union for life.

At middle age, a grieving mother
who lost four of seven children.
She knew the cost
to slave mothers who lost
their children to the auction block.

Harriet Beecher Stowe . . .

A woman whose convictions
became frozen in time
like a photograph in a frame,
her opposition to slavery would claim
the rest of her life.

At age forty-one
she wrote *Uncle Tom's Cabin*,
of lives bruised and crushed
by slavery that must
be abolished.

Her brutal tale admired by
Eliot, Holmes,
Dickens and Twain,
exposed the shameful stain
of slavery on the nation.

At her death
a simple tribute called her book
"The spark that started the war."
Had she known that beforehand
she might have written more.

SEARCHING FOR WOUNDED SOLDIERS

Mary Ann Bickerdyke
1817 - 1901
She searched battlefields for wounded
Union soldiers left for dead

They gathered in a small white church.
Children squirmed, the sermon was long.
The pastor paused, a letter in hand,
injured Union troops needed help,
Who would go?
Mary Ann.

Saying goodbye to family and friends,
she boarded a train to Cairo town,
and found diseased and wounded soldiers
among the filth and stench,
and every one a dying man.
Who would care for them?
Mary Ann.

They came by the hundreds,
frozen and mangled men,
chilled to the bone, burning with fever,
raging in delirium, faint with loss of blood.
Who met the flood?
Mary Ann.

Mary Ann Bickerdyke . . .

She cleaned and cooked
and begged and borrowed supplies,
and angered doctors by flaunting authority
for the men in her care.
Mary Ann
Was everywhere!

She followed Grant's army
down the mighty Mississippi.
Like renegade mushrooms
hospitals sprung up with lightning speed,
sandbags against the flood of wounded.
Who met the need?
Mary Ann.

Little by little
a few were well enough to leave,
but others took their places.
And she walked the silent battlefields at night
by lantern light,
listening for the slightest sound
from the lips of a wounded man.
Who would hear them?
Mary Ann.

SPYING FOR THE CONFEDERACY

Rose O'Neal Greenhow
1817 - 1864
A Washington hostess who
passed Yankee secrets to the South

They call me Union traitor
for the spying that I do.
I'm a woman and a widow
and a loving mother, too.
You won't find a better hostess
in all of Washington,
Sending Yankee secrets to the South
until the war is won.
The Pinkertons have placed me
under strictest house arrest.
But I manage to get messages
to the agents I know best.
Then I'm hurried off to prison,
with just time to pack a bag.
But from my prison window
see me wave the Southern flag.
In the North I am a traitor
In the South, a hero when
regardless of the consequences
I'd do it all again.

FIGHTING UNJUST LAWS

Elizabeth Cady Stanton 1815 - 1902
Fighter for Women's Rights

Elizabeth lived in an age
when women could not own property,
had no rights over their children,
could be beaten by their husbands,
and not allowed to keep an earned wage.

Young Elizabeth heard many a tale
in her father's law office
of mistreated women who had lost
their children and had no place to turn.
(The laws were on the side of the male.)

Elizabeth believed if she cut the laws
out of her father's books,
they would be canceled forever.
But it didn't work that way,
so she took up her lifelong cause.

Elizabeth fought for women her entire life,
organized the first women's convention,
spoke for a woman's right to vote
and wrote for newspapers and magazines
demanding equal laws for husband and wife.

Elizabeth did not live to see
her goals become reality.
To achieve her ends
she aroused strong feelings in both
enemies and friends,
but her work paved the way for victory.

FREE AT LAST!

Lizzie Keckley 1818 - 1907
A former slave who became the confidant of
Mary Todd Lincoln

In eighteen hundred eighteen
a girl slave was born before
slaves would gain their freedom.
Put to work when she was four
watching the new baby
till the cradle tipped, and CRASH!
the little one pitched to the floor
and Lizzie felt the lash.
Lizzie's mother was a seamstress
and her Master's clan of ten
kept her nimble fingers flying,
too much work for her, and then
Lizzie rendered her assistance.
She learned to cut and sew.
Working late into the night
by the yellow lantern's glow.

Lizzie's father and her mother
loved her dearly and full well,
till the Master with a letter
in his hand, came to tell
that her father had been sold
to another traveling west.
There was nothing to be done.
There was no way to protest

Lizzie Keckley . . .

The announcement like an arrow
tore through her mother's heart
and brought tears and sobs of anguish
knowing soon that they must part.
Wild in thought but chained in action
Lizzie dreamed of being free.
Sent a solemn prayer to heaven
for an end to slavery.

At fourteen she was sent to work
in the household of a son.
Did the work of three and
scolded if a job was left undone.
The scoldings turned to beatings
to subdue her "stubborn pride."
The girl stood like a statue
while the lashes cut her side.
Lizzie now a grown woman
bore a son. Then a return
to the Virginia Master's household
where she was surprised to learn
of a new life in St. Louis.
But the family was so poor
that she sought work to support them
by going door to door.

Lizzie Keckley . . .

She never lacked for orders
from the ladies of the town.
Then she married Mr. Keckley
in her self-made wedding gown.
But her husband was no helpmate.
When he told her he was free,
a falsehood had been uttered
as she was soon to see.

Eight years passed, then her Master
said that freedom she might buy
if she had one hundred dollars
times twelve to multiply.
Somehow she'd raise the money
to claim a free birthright.
To help her came a patron
like a ray of bright sunlight,
who brought her the twelve hundred
gathered from a host of friends.
"FREE at last," cried Lizzie Keckley.
"This life of bondage ends!"

Lizzie paid back the twelve hundred,
traveled then to Washington.
Set herself up as a seamstress
and gained patrons one by one.

Lizzie Keckley . . .

When the President's wife spilled coffee
on her best inaugural dress,
who was called to sew another?
No need to take a guess.
Lizzie Keckley sewed a gown
with her hard-won expertise
that impressed Mrs. Lincoln,
a woman hard to please.

Mrs. Lincoln trusted Lizzie
with her secrets and her fears.
Shared her inner thoughts and dreams,
shared her laughter and her tears.
Lizzie came to be a confidant
on whom she could depend.
Former slave, now the First Lady's
most true and trusted friend.

THE FIRST WOMAN DOCTOR

Elizabeth Blackwell 1821 - 1910
America's first woman doctor

Elizabeth hated the word, NO!
NO money
meant poverty at the age of ten.
NO career
(professions were only for men.)
NO encouragement
in her wish to be a physician.
NO! NO! NO!
when she applied for admission.
NO school,
except one, (took her on probation.)
NO woman
could see a live demonstration.
NO friendship
with others who were quick to harass.
NO cheers
when she graduated, first in her class.
NO stopping
her starting a medical school.
NO standards
too high, hard work was the rule.
NO woman
rejected who was willing to try.
NO place
for a man who might choose to apply.
NO wonder
this woman holds the position
of America's first trained woman physician.

TRICKING A GENERAL

Mary Ann Harris Gay 1829 - 1918
A Southern spy in petticoats who found ways to
hide Confederate uniforms

A woman of strong conviction,
her soft-spoken Southern diction
allowed her to outsmart
the Yankee General who had a part
in commandeering her home and land,
not knowing that she had a hand
in smuggling goods and information
along to each Confederate station.

When brother, Thomie, asked to hide
uniforms, it was with pride
she knocked a hole in the attic wall,
and hid them all.
(Said the hole was made by a cannonball).

When winter dropped the first snowflake,
Mary knew that she must take
the warmer clothes to freezing men.
An idea came to her, and then
saying a relative was sick, packed a wagon,
told the General goodbye (another trick)
and just before the winter storms
delivered those warm uniforms.

DEFENDING WORKER'S RIGHTS

Mother Jones (Mary Harris Jones)
1830 - 1930
Her efforts improved conditions and wages for workers

Mary Harris Jones was old.
At ninety-three she still was bold as brass!
She'd hop right on the nearest train,
put on her hat and go raise cain.
She had no home, no money, no kin
but was interested in
the worker's plight.
She traveled north and east and west
exhorting men to do their best.
To hold out in their strikers' lines
against the owners of the mines.
Some of the hardships that she tells
were cold and hunger, cat-call yells,
food with maggots, danger near,
and worst of all, the constant fear
that she might fail.
"Take her away," the owners said.
"Prison's what she needs instead."
This woman's never-ending fight
against the workers' awful plight
brought her close to death at times
from owners' guns at strikers' lines.
Hated by one, revered by the other
This is the tale of feisty Mother Jones.

MEDAL OF HONOR

Mary Edwards Walker 1832 - 1919
A woman physician in the Civil War,
recipient of the Medal of Honor

A woman physician in 1861
who wore a surgeon's hat
and pants instead of skirts?
Unthinkable!
BUT TRUE!

A woman surgeon
in the Union Army
healing men wounded in battle?
Preposterous!
BUT TRUE!

A woman prisoner
who told Confederates goodbye,
when exchanged for another?
Impossible!
BUT TRUE!

Awarded the Medal of Honor,
the first given to a woman
for meritorious service to her country?
Unbelievable!
BUT TRUE!

CONQUERING THE ART WORLD

Mary Cassatt 1844?(45?) - 1926
A woman who took her place among the
foremost of American painters

She fought a world
that said artists were men
and found the French impressionists,
but made their art and ideas her own,
no imitator was she,
her style light and free.

At first she painted
a woman reading in a garden,
a toreador, a lamp and a woman in black,
by golden light
colors blended, gentle and mild
bringing to life mother and child.

Later she painted
smudges on herself as well as her plates,
colors clear and boldly defined.
From hand to brush to print
images appeared.
Art critics cheered.

20

CRUSADING FOR ENDANGERED WILDLIFE

Elizabeth Knight Britton 1858 - 1934
A botanist who fought to save wildlife

It is a fact that
Elizabeth Britton
had a love
for growing things.
With practiced eye
above the lens
she shared plant secrets
with those who cared
as she did.

It is a fact that
one day Elizabeth
looked around
at barren ground
in the Bronx.
Told city fathers,
"I beg your pardon
but you need a garden
for all the people
to enjoy."

It is a fact that
Elizabeth Britton
was not afraid
to start a crusade for
endangered wildlife.
She spent many hours
saving trees and flowers.
A woman who would plead
for all to see the need
as she did.

Calamity Jane (Martha Jane Canary)
1848?(52?) - 1903
Army scout and Pony Express rider

What will I be?

Wife? Teacher? Nurse?

Not me!

Army scout

Handy with a gun.

Pony Express rider

when the war was won.

Deadwood to Custer,

danger on the trail.

Outlaws tried,

but didn't get the mail.

Fast mount

Quick shot

100-mile ride,

Never lost a letter,

would have hurt my pride.

With positive opinions

of what a gal can be,

The nickname

that they gave me

It fits!

CALAMITY

FIGHTING SEGREGATION

Mary Church Terrell 1863 - 1954
A leader in the fight against segregation

The laws in D.C. in 1873 required restaurants
to serve any person regardless of race,
and if not, to face
a thousand dollar fine.

But the law was revised in 1890
when it was arranged
that the rules be changed.
People of color were no longer served.

Then came a woman of wealth,
with a wagonload of courage
determined to discourage
segregation in all of its forms.

This former teacher of eighty-plus years
launched a campaign
to peacefully complain
with sit-ins, boycotts and picketing.

And because of her work,
the laws were struck down
As of June 8, 1953,
persons of any race were free
to dine wherever they wished.

SMASHING THE OIL TRUSTS

Ida Tarbell 1857 - 1944
A woman journalist who brought down
the Rockefeller Oil Empire

America in 1880, a land of plenty
where the rich wanted more
ignoring the poor
to line their overflowing pockets.

Enter a young journalist
whose father had been undercut
by ruthless oil barons, and shut
out of his business.

She took on the rich oil giants
with the written word,
then the nation heard
of strong arm tactics
and price gouging.

She wrote about an oil empire
that used force as tools
as it broke all the rules
to smash the small competitor.

Her series shocked her readers
who demanded the courts must
put an end to oil trusts,
AND THEY DID!

CHALLENGING JULES VERNE

Elizabeth Cochrane (Nellie Bly)
1867 - 1922
She went around the world in 72 days!

In Apollo, Pennsylvania
Elizabeth was five when she
dreamed of traveling widely
as she watched the trains arrive.

Encouraged to be curious
she read and read and learned
and at the age of nineteen,
her living to be earned.

Left home for the big city
where a news piece caught her eye.
It made her mad, and so she chose
to pen a terse reply.

It said that girls should stay at home
and not seek a career.
In her reply, Elizabeth
made her position clear.

Nellie Bly . . .

The editor was so impressed
at how this girl could write,
he offered her a reporter's job
much to her delight.

For in eighteen hundred eighty three
reporters were all men.
Elizabeth would do her job
in a virtual lion's den.

But the brave girl took the challenge
looked reporters in the eye
and proceeded to introduce herself
as Reporter, Nellie Bly!

She wrote of cruel treatment
of the mentally insane
by getting herself committed
to see first-hand the shame

of the brutal beatings given
to the afflicted and the worn.
She wrote about the doctors
with derision and with scorn.

Her reporting shocked the public
who demanded things be changed,
that there be humane treatment
of the mentally deranged.

Nellie Bly . . .

Investigative journalist
at only twenty-three
Nellie was a pioneer
who happened then to see

A book by author, Jules Verne,
Around the World in 80 Days
"I'll do it in less time," she said
"by avoiding long delays."

So she hopped right on a steamer,
and she traveled some by train
to Ireland, Paris, France and Greece,
Russia, the Ukraine,

Singapore and China,
her list of countries grew.
And it did not take her eighty days,
but only seventy-two.

She's remembered as a fighter,
her sword, the written word.
When something needed fixing
she made sure the people heard.

Nellie fought for those less fortunate.
She did the job with flair
Best Reporter in America,
Nellie made the public care.

STARTING A SCHOOL WITH $1.50

Mary McLeod Bethune 1875 - 1955
With determination and hard work
she built a school

She had a dream
to build a school
for those who lived
in tarpaper shacks
and among the trash dumps.

With $1.50 she raised rent money.
Would sell her hat
if that would help.
Scoured junk yards
for anything usable,
Made ink from berries,
pencils from charred wood.

She scrubbed and cleaned.
She fixed up and she taught
those first five students,
and in between she twisted
the arms of businessmen.

Five students grew to one hundred.
Five dollars down bought the land.
She said goodbye to that one room,
and built a building
five stories tall.
She had a dream to build a school,
and she did!

28

SAVING LIVES AT SEA

Molly (Margaret) Tobin Brown 1867 - 1932
A brave woman who saved lives when the *Titanic* sank

CRASH! SCRAPE! RIP! TEAR!
Like the seam of a poorly made garment
the *Titanic* split apart,
cut by iceberg scissors.

WAILS! MOANS! CRIES! SCREAMS!
The ship tilts, a dancer losing her balance.
A stampede of bodies crowding the rails.
Women and children go first.

SWELL! SPLASH! SLAP! POUND!
The waves reach out like a hungry beast,
anticipating a tasty meal
with lifeboats for dessert.

PULL! ROW! GET AWAY! GET AWAY!
Angered at a useless, shivering sailor,
Molly Brown grabs the oars,
a captain in chinchilla fur.

ROW! SING! ROW! SING!
The women sang and rowed to safety.
A symphony of courage
conducted by a woman
who wouldn't give up.

WRESTLING THE GRAND CANYON

Mary Elizabeth Colter 1869 - 1958
The woman architect, who in 1905, designed and
built many structures still standing today at the
Grand Canyon

Designing buildings on the rim of the Grand Canyon is like a

wrestling match with the Earth.

On one side of the circle, a blue-eyed Yankee girl who said

goodbye to Pennsylvania to live in a wild land.

On the other, the harsh canyon landscape,

made of rocks, cliffs, ridges, hills and valleys of every form.

Looking for leverage, the girl studies her opponent,

takes its measure and begins to sketch.

Here comes a take-down as a building rises,

then another and another,

Phantom Ranch, Hopi House, the Watchtower.

Testing the architect's ability,

the canyon tries a sit out, hiding its secrets to escape holds.

But the girl is sharp-eyed.

Not a single building stone escapes her inspection

and she uses only the best.

Maintaining a position of advantage, a fall is scored.

She makes peace with the land

with structures of natural wonder

that blend perfectly with the spectacular setting.

The match is ended.

CLAIMING THE SKY

Bessie Coleman 1892?(96?) - 1926
The first African-American woman pilot

Bessie Coleman
had a love
for the birds of the air
and longed to go where
they did.
But no matter how hard she tried
she was denied
entrance to flying schools
because she was black.

Bessie Coleman
worked hard and
with the money she earned
went to France and learned
to fly.
She was the first of her race
To take her place
among the best-known pilots
of the world.

Bessie Coleman
flew without fear
barnstormer, stunt flyer
her fame grew higher and higher!
Queen Bess!
A woman who would call
for opportunities for all
to achieve their dream
as she did.

BECOMING THE WORLD'S CONSCIENCE

Eleanor Roosevelt
1884 - 1962
A First Lady Who Fought for the Rights of People Everywhere

How To Be a First Lady

Study languages and literature for twenty years

Excel in compassion for fellow humans

Have an uncle who becomes president

Make sure you are Franklin's fifth cousin

Visit slums to gain firsthand knowledge of the poor

Take public speaking lessons

Argue with lawmakers over equal rights for women

Write for a newspaper

Hold women-only press conferences

Ignore the latest fashion trends

Be a thorn in the side of those who pay lip
service to human rights

Say to those who advise you to retire from
public life
NEVER!
NEVER!
NEVER!

THE LITTLE COLONEL

Mary A. Hallaren
1907 -
The highly respected Third Director of the
Women's Army Corps

She was one woman

who said goodbye to home and answered the call.

One among many who

volunteered to serve so a world could be free.

She was one officer

who earned honors and medallions.

Leader of World War II WAAC battalions

9000 strong, across the Atlantic Sea.

She was a tiny giant

the "Little Colonel," a name of affection

given by her troops for her wise direction,

who came home with honors, a V.I.P.

WINNING THE GOLD

Elizabeth (Betty) Robinson Schwartz
1911 - 1999
Won two Olympic Gold Medals in track, the second
after being severely injured in a plane crash

1928

With an athlete's body

she runs the race.

Fast track, feet fly,

she sets the pace.

And wins an Olympic Gold.

1931

Plane crash! Injured body

slow to heal.

Twisted spine, stiff joints

like a new shoe might feel

needing to be broken in.

1936

With an athlete's body

she runs the relay.

Feet fly, baton pass

in the race to stay

and another Olympic Gold!

FLYING FREE

Mary Martin
1913 - 1990
A young dance teacher takes on Hollywood and Broadway

What happened when Mary wanted to be a boy?

Did she fall off a trapeze?

Mess up her best dress?

Step off a garage roof?

YES!

What happened when Mary wanted to sing?

Did she sing everywhere she went?

Sing at the local firemen's dinner?

And wish she could slide down the fire pole?

YES!

What happened when Mary had to earn a living?

Did she take dance lessons?

Open a dance studio?

See her studio burn down?

YES!

Mary Martin . . .

What happened when Mary said goodbye

to Texas and went to Hollywood?

Did she audition for every singing part?

Wow a crowd at a talent show?

Perform in films and on Broadway?

YES!

What happened when Mary wanted to be a boy?

Did she play the part of Peter Pan?

Fly through the air with a feather in her hat?

And get her wish to slide down a fire pole?

YES! YES! YES!

FIGHTING THE DRUG COMPANIES

Frances Oldham Kelsey 1914 -
The doctor who kept Thalidomide from
sales in the United States

The drug company called her STUBBORN!
For her procrastination
in approving a medication
by the Food and Drug Administration.
(She asked for more information.)

The drug company called her STUPID!
When in anticipation
of big sales throughout the nation
saw no reason for hesitation.
(Said it was discrimination.)

The drug company called her
UNREASONABLE!
Until new revelations
from a host of European nations
cited birth defects in the generation
whose mothers took the medication.

The nation called her a HEROINE!
Who risked her reputation
in withholding the recommendation
with every justification.
The medication?
THALIDOMIDE

TAKING ON THE CORPORATE WORLD

Mary Kathlyn Ash (Mary Kay) D. 2001
She built a successful business with
hard work and an "I can do!" attitude

There she is,

standing above the crowd,

fair skin, sparkling eyes, beauty personified.

Helping women to make dreams come true,

"YOU CAN DO IT!" she shouts.

There she is,

a child with invalid father and working mother,

cooking, cleaning, shopping.

A heavy burden for a seven-year-old.

"YOU CAN DO IT!" her mother tells her.

There she is,

Sole support of three children,

who stumbled on a beauty secret

and said goodbye to hard times.

Woman business owner in a man's world.

"YOU CAN DO IT!" she tells herself.

There she is,

smiling and waving to a cheering crowd.

Queen of a beauty empire

telling women that they CAN do it,

"AS I DID!" she says.

FIGHTING FOR MIGRANT WORKERS

Delores Huerta 1930 -
She led the fight to improve farm workers' lives

What did she do
when her parents divorced
poverty reigned
opportunities were few?
She excelled in her studies.

What did she do
when she saw injustice
knew the helplessness of the poor
saw the power of education?
She got a college degree.

What did she do
when migrant workers lived in hovels
received poor wages for their work
had to pay for a drink of water?
She led the protest.
Taught citizenship classes.
Encouraged workers to vote.
Led boycotts and picket lines.
Raised funds.
Advised government leaders.

What did she do
When she was beaten in a demonstration
Nearly lost her life
Spent months in recovery?
She did it all over again!

VAULTING TO FAME

Mary Lou Retton 1968 -
The first American woman to win an
Olympic gold medal in gymnastics

She began with dance and
acrobatics at the age of four.
All eyes were on the floor
where she performed
and charmed.

Next came gymnastics
With a style suited
to her compact muscular frame.
She excelled at the game.
The young star
would go far.

She entered tournaments
and went to Japan
to enter competition while
showing a most unique style.
She was up
for the Chunichi Cup.

Then came the Olympics where
She executed the
exceptionally difficult Tsukahara vault
a perfect back somersault.
Tiny but bold
she won the gold!

SPACE WOMAN

Mary Ellen Weber
1962 -
Who logged over 450 hours in space successfully
delivering into orbit a critical NASA communications
satellite

Recipe for an Astronaut

TAKE

One measure talented student

With a Ph.D. in chemical engineering

Blend in revolutionary ideas for computers

with a Silver Medal in the U.S. National Skydiving

Championships

Add science training of NASA crews

Mix spacecraft with

One female astronaut complete with helmet

Telling planet Earth goodbye

On two hard-working missions

Flying a sixty-foot robotic arm

And directing the transfer of 3000 pounds of equipment

Process for a total of 450 hours

Preserve Mary Ellen Weber as an American

woman veteran of spaceflight.

BIOGRAPHICAL SKETCHES

Molly Pitcher (Mary Hays McCauly) 1753 - 1832

Married at age fifteen, Molly Hays lived with her husband in a small Pennsylvania town until a call came from General Washington for men to serve in the Continental Army. Artillery wives often traveled with their husbands to cook for them between battles.

On June 28, 1778, young Mary Hays, often called Molly, brought pitchers of water to battle weary, thirsty men engaged in the Battle of Monmouth. It was a blistering hot day and Molly responded as quickly as she could to cries of "Molly, Molly, over here!" When her husband fell wounded there was no one to man the cannon until Molly ran forward and picked up the rammer staff. She stayed at her post throughout the battle despite the heavy enemy fire. For her bravery, George Washington issued her a warrant as a noncommissioned officer. After this, the troops affectionately called her "Sergeant Molly."

Elizabeth (Betty) Zane 1766 - 1831

Betty Zane lived in Wheeling, Virginia (now West Virginia), a town founded in 1759 by her brothers. When in September 1792, Indians attacked the town, all of the residents took shelter in Fort Henry. However, their supply of gunpowder was low, and to obtain more powder someone would have to run fifty yards in front of the enemy to the house where they stored the powder.

Although there is no solid evidence of the heroism of Betty Zane, legend tells that she volunteered to get the needed powder. She ran the fifty yards while the Indians simply watched, but when they saw her returning with the gun powder, they opened fire. She was not injured and delivered the powder safely. Her brave act saved the fort by enabling the men to hold off the attackers until help arrived. She later moved to Ohio, married twice and had seven children.

Dolley Payne Todd Madison 1768 - 1849

Born in 1768 in North Carolina, Dolley Payne was raised in a strict Quaker family. When she was one year old, the family moved to Philadelphia. At age twenty-two she married John Todd, Jr. who died three years later leaving Dolley and a young son. The young widow met and fell in love with James Madison, who was seventeen years older than she. They were married in 1794 and Madison became president in 1809. Dolley had the social graces and political know-how to be a perfect president's wife and was widely admired.

In 1812 when the British army was approaching Washington, Dolley refused to leave the White House until most of its national treasures were loaded on wagons and taken away. The famous painting of George Washington by Gilbert Stuart was among these. Driving one of the carriages herself, she took none of her personal belongings but made sure that they saved the White House artifacts that belonged to all of the people. Following his Presidency, the Madisons retired to their plantation in Virginia where James Madison died in 1836. Dolley moved back to Washington and spent the remainder of her life there.

Elizabeth Kortright Monroe 1768 - 1830

Born in New York City, Elizabeth Kortright was the daughter of a privateer who made his fortune during the French and Indian Wars. At age seventeen Elizabeth married James Monroe, a veteran with political ambitions.

In 1794 President Washington appointed Monroe Minister to France and Elizabeth accompanied him there. The French Revolution was in full force and Elizabeth discovered that the wife of Lafayette was in prison and was to be put to death on the guillotine. Elizabeth went to the prison and asked to visit the woman. Because of her visit, the woman was set free. James Monroe became president in 1817 and while Elizabeth was an excellent hostess, ill health forced her to take a less active role as First Lady. The Monroes retired to their plantation in Oak Hill where she died in 1830 at 62.

Harriet Beecher Stowe 1811 - 1896

Born in 1811, Harriet was the daughter of an abolitionist preacher, one of thirteen children. Her mother died when she was four. In 1836 she married Calvin Stowe, a minister also opposed to slavery. Harriet and Calvin sheltered fugitive slaves in their home until they moved to Maine in 1850. After losing four of her seven children, Harriet knew the deep loss felt by slave mothers when their children were sold from them. At the age of forty-one she wrote <u>Uncle Tom's Cabin</u> that was labeled "the spark that started the Civil War."

Mary Ann (Mother) Bickerdyke 1817 - 1901

In 1861, Mary Ann Bickerdyke, a widow with two children, volunteered to take medical supplies to the wounded in Cairo, Illinois, and to report on needs of the troops. Conditions were appalling and she decided to stay and care for the wounded. For the next four years she nursed the wounded in nineteen major battles, often angering doctors in her demands for better conditions and supplies. When food was scarce, she was known to travel great distances to obtain it for "her boys." She often walked the battlefields at night, lantern in hand, listening for the cries of wounded who might have been left behind. For her untiring work she received the respect and admiration of thousands of soldiers and was called Mother Bickerdyke by them. General Sherman gave her the greatest accolade with the simple words "She outranks me."

Rose O'Neal Greenhow 1817 - 1864

In 1835, Rose Greenhow became one of Washington D. C.'s most popular hostesses. When the Civil War began, she used her gifts to gain military information to pass on to the South. She was put under house arrest by Pinkerton detectives and later sent to a prison. In 1862 she was released with warnings never to return to the North. In 1863, in order to obtain much needed funds for the Confederacy, she sailed to Europe where she was well received. She lost her life in 1864 dodging Union gunboats when her small boat overturned in a violent storm.

Elizabeth Cady Stanton 1815 - 1902

Born in Johnstown, New York, Elizabeth was educated at
what is now the Emma Willard School. As a child in her father's
law office she saw the injustice suffered by many women who
had, by law, no rights over their children, their money or their
physical well being should their husbands decide to beat them.
Her marriage in 1840 to Henry Stanton allowed her to attend
the international slavery convention in London with him. They
did not allow women, however, to speak at the convention.
Considering this another great injustice, she devoted her life to
obtaining equality for women. She was president of the
National Women's Suffrage Association and the National
American Woman Suffrage Association. She edited a magazine
and coauthored a series of books about her cause. Her work
made her both friends and enemies as it paved the way for
equality in the law for women.

Lizzie (Elizabeth) Hobbs Keckley 1818 - 1907

Born a slave, Lizzie Keckley worked hard all her life. She
endured beatings when tasks were not done to her master's
liking but was encouraged by her mother to be the best that she
could be. Her father was sold away from the plantation when
Lizzie was a child. As an excellent seamstress she served her
master well, at one time supporting the family by taking sewing
jobs for other families. She married in 1852 but soon
discovered she had been deceived. Her husband posed as a free
man when he was not and he was an alcoholic. With the help of
friends that she later paid back, she bought her freedom for
$1200.00. Lizzie set up her own business and started a school
for young black girls. She became not only the personal
dressmaker but a friend and confidant to Mary Todd Lincoln.
The friendship ended with the publication of her book, Behind
the Scenes, about the life of Mrs. Lincoln and events in the
White House. She died in obscurity in 1907.

Elizabeth Blackwell 1821 - 1910

Born in England, Elizabeth came to the United States
with her parents when she was twelve. When she was
seventeen, her father died and Elizabeth and her sisters
supported the family by running a boarding school. She
continued to teach but studied medicine at the same time.
Desiring formal training in medicine, she wrote to many
medical schools but was rejected by all until she received
acceptance from the Geneva Medical School in New York.
Even then, because she was a woman, she was not allowed
to observe live demonstrations. After two years of study
she graduated with high honors.

She continued her studies at LaMaternité Hospital where
she contracted an infection that left her blind in one eye.
Again, because of her sex she was turned down for several
positions, so she set up her own practice with her sister.
It later became the New York Infirmary and College for
Women. Later in her life she returned to London where she
continued to practice medicine and became a professor at
the London School of Medicine for Women.

Mary Ann Harris Gay 1829 - 1918

Mary Ann was a strong Southern woman who refused to
leave her home when Union troops took it over. When her
brother asked her to hide Confederate uniforms, she
knocked a hole in the parlor ceiling and hid them in the
attic. She told the general that a cannonball had done the
damage.

Mary Ann later delivered the uniforms by tricking the
Union general out of a wagon and horses. To buy food for
hungry children, she searched battlefields for bullets that
they could melt down and sell. After the war she raised
money to rebuild a church and to preserve a Confederate
soldiers' cemetery. She gained fame with her book <u>Life in
Dixie During the War</u>.

Mary Harris Jones 1830 - 1930

Arriving in Canada as an immigrant from Ireland in 1835, Mary trained to be a teacher but gave up teaching after eight months saying she was not going to spend her life "bossing little children." In 1861 she married George E. Jones, an iron worker who had strong views about the rights of workers. In 1867 while living in Memphis, Tennessee, Mary lost her husband and four children in the yellow fever epidemic. She moved to Chicago where she became active in the labor movement.

Her life's work was helping immigrants and farmers who were forced to work for starvation wages. She encouraged workers to strike, bringing whatever help she could. She gave strong speeches about the plight of child workers. While participating in a coal miners' strike at age 83 she was convicted of murder and sentenced to 20 years in prison but was freed by the governor. She continued to speak out against injustices for workers well into her nineties and on her 100th birthday gave a rousing speech before cameras. She died seven months after her 100th birthday.

Mary Edwards Walker 1832 - 1919

The only woman in United States history to receive the Congressional Medal of Honor, Mary Walker was one of the first women doctors to graduate from Syracuse Medical College. She had a difficult time practicing medicine in Rome, New York, since women physicians were not accepted by the citizens. With the coming of the Civil War she enlisted in the Union Army where she worked as a surgeon in field hospitals. At the same time she crossed Confederate lines to treat civilians and to bring back vital information. She was taken prisoner in 1864 and spent four months in a Confederate prison.

She received the Congressional Medal of Honor from President Andrew Jackson. It was revoked, along with many others in 1917, but restored by presidential order in 1977. Mary Walker defied conventions of her time by wearing men's clothing, and after the war she continued to lecture for social reform.

Mary Cassatt 1844?(45?) - 1926

In an age when the art world belonged to men, Mary Cassatt was determined to become an artist. Not only did she reach this goal but she is considered one of America's foremost printmakers of the nineteenth century. She first studied art at the Pennsylvania Academy of Fine Arts. In 1865 she traveled to Europe where she studied in Madrid, Rome, and Paris. Her work was rejected over and over in Salon exhibitions and juried shows.

It was then that she met Edgar Degas who invited her to join the Impressionists and submit work for a new print journal. Producing prints was painstaking work, and the series of ten prints that she did in 1891 was a major achievement and led to her acceptance in the art world as a major artist. Though she spent most of her life in Europe, America claims her as its own. Before blindness prevented her from working in 1911, she produced more than 200 prints.

Elizabeth Britton 1858 - 1934

From childhood Elizabeth had a passionate interest in wild things. Her fascination with plants led her to study botany, and she became known as a leading authority in the field. Her education at Hunter College led her to become an expert on mosses, and she became director of the moss collection at Columbia University.

One of her major concerns was the disappearance of wildlife as civilization brought about larger cities. Realizing city people had no place to go to enjoy wildlife, she was responsible for talking the leaders of the Bronx into providing land and funds for The New York Botanical Garden, a 250-acre site that can be visited today. She founded the Wildflower Preservation Society in 1898 and led movements that saved 100s of endangered species.

Martha Jane Canary (Calamity Jane) 1848?(52?) - 1903

Born in Princeton, Missouri, Martha moved to Nevada with her father and brothers a few years after the death of her mother. Following an Indian uprising when she was separated from her family, Martha found herself on her own at age ten. She survived through toughness and determination. She learned to ride and shoot as well as any man. Before age twenty she became an army scout serving with Buffalo Bill. Canary moved around a great deal and in 1876, rode for the Pony Express. Her route was one of the roughest in the Black Hills Country but her reputation as a marksman got her through safely. More travels saw her working to build new forts and towns, ranching and prospecting. In the Dakota territories she saved the lives of many Deadwood citizens by nursing them through a smallpox epidemic. She married in Texas and had one daughter. Then she returned to Deadwood where old and new friends alike greeted her warmly as the Woman Scout who helped to tame the West.

Mary Church Terrell 1863 - 1954

Mary was born into a wealthy family and was one of the first black women to receive a college degree. She continued her studies in Europe and became fluent in many languages. She became a teacher but was forced to resign upon her marriage to Robert Terrell in 1891. Her deep interest in stopping segregation in all its forms led to her founding of the National Association of Colored Women. In her post as president she worked tirelessly to end discrimination. In 1872 laws passed in the District of Columbia prevented restaurant owners from discriminating against people of color. By 1950 the laws had been abandoned, and in her late eighties Mary Terrell began a campaign to reinstate the laws. At age 91 she led a restaurant sit-in. When refused service, Mary and her companions filed a lawsuit while continuing to picket other restaurants. The suit was successful, and they declared segregated restaurants unconstitutional. She continued her work into her nineties as one of the founders of NAACP's Executive Committee.

Ida Tarbell 1857 - 1944

Growing up around the Pennsylvania oil fields, Ida often heard hard luck tales from those who had lost their land and oil wells to the strong-arm tactics of the Rockefeller empire. Her father, who manufactured wooden oil tanks, lost his business when his prices were undercut by the Rockefellers.

After being educated in the United States, Ida Tarbell went to France to continue her studies. While there, she interviewed notables and sent copies of her interviews to *McClure's Magazine*. She later became a member of the magazine's staff where her articles were well received. Painstaking research into the oil industry and the unethical tactics of the Rockefellers led to a series of articles that exposed the ruthless practices of the Standard Oil Trust that controlled 95% of all the oil produced in the United States. Her series led Congress to investigate and to pass the Sherman Anti-Trust Act.

Elizabeth Cochrane (Nellie Bly) 1867 - 1922

The first woman to gain fame as an investigative journalist, Elizabeth Cochrane was willing to put herself in danger if it meant a good story. She got her first job as a reporter by writing a letter of protest. The letter so impressed the paper's editor that he hired Elizabeth and gave her her pen name, Nellie Bly.

To investigate conditions in mental institutions she managed to have herself committed to see the horrors first hand. Further stories exposed poverty, strikes, poor medical care, treatment of women by police, corruption and injustice. In 1889 to beat the record of the hero in Jules Verne's Around the World in Eighty Days, she went around the world in seventy-two days. She married in 1897 and ran her husband's business after his death.

Mary McLeod Bethune 1875 - 1955

Born in South Carolina, one of seventeen children to parents who were former slaves, Mary had her first chance to go to school when a school was opened for African-American children four miles from her home. She was such a good student her teacher recommended her for a scholarship to Scotia Academy where she again excelled. After continuing her education at the Moody Bible Institute, she taught for two years until her marriage to Albettus Bethune in 1898.

After the birth of her son she accepted a call from a Florida preacher to teach in a mission school. She saw a great need for educational opportunities for black children. With no money but great determination she started a school with five pupils. The school was a success, and as enrollment grew she was able to find a permanent home for it. As the years passed it became Bethune-Cookman College. Her successes became nationally recognized, and she was appointed to several government positions including Director of the Division of Negro Affairs of the National Youth Administration. She also served on the United States delegation to develop the United Nations Charter.

Molly (Margaret) Tobin Brown 1867 - 1932

Molly was born in Hannibal, Missouri, one of six children of poor Irish immigrants. As a young woman she worked as a waitress, then went to Colorado where she met and married James J. Brown and had two children. In 1912 Molly Brown, while touring Europe, boarded the *Titanic* to return to the United States where her grandson was gravely ill.

On day five of the voyage, the ship hit an iceberg and began to sink. Molly was thrown into a lifeboat with 14 other women and a sailor who told them they were sure to die, for when the *Titanic* went down it would pull them down with it. Molly took charge and got the women singing and rowing, and they were eventually picked up by a rescue ship, the *Carpathia*. She organized rescue efforts on the ship and raised money for victims of the disaster. When asked by reporters how she was able to survive the disaster she stated that she was "unsinkable."

Mary Elizabeth Jane Colter 1869 - 1958

They said it couldn't be done, that the terrain was too rough to build permanent structures in and around the Grand Canyon. Yet, over 32 years, a young, talented and determined woman designed and supervised the building of Hopi House, Hermit's Rest, Lookout Studio, Phantom Ranch, The Watchtower and Bright Angel Lodge.

After persuading her family to allow her to attend the California School of Design, she taught in Michigan until 1901 when the Fred Harvey Company hired her to decorate a hotel in Albuquerque. This was followed by commissions for the buildings in the Grand Canyon where she integrated her original ideas with Native American designs. As one of the few female architects of her time, Mary Colter had to fight for recognition by designing and constructing buildings as perfect as they could be. No detail was too small to be ignored. She designed and decorated buildings for the Harvey Company for 40 years, and her work can be seen today throughout the Southwest.

Bessie Coleman (Queen Bess) 1892?(96?) - 1926

As a young woman Bessie was determined to learn to fly but was denied entry to flying schools in the United States. With the financial help of two African-American businessmen, Bessie went to France and became the first American woman to obtain a pilot's license.

She returned to the United States and performed in air shows as a barnstormer, parachutist and stunt flyer where she earned the name Queen Bess. Her goal was to save enough money to open a flight school for black pilots, male and female. She lost her life on a test flight when the plane turned upside down and she was thrown out without the parachute she usually wore.

Eleanor Roosevelt 1884 - 1962

Eleanor was a shy child who lost her mother when she was eight years old and was sent to live with her grandmother, a strict woman not known for her warmth. She excelled in academics and gained confidence in her abilities after studying in France with an encouraging teacher. In 1905 she married Franklin D. Roosevelt who was later to become president of the United States.

Eleanor became his eyes and ears as she traveled the country, seeing first hand the extreme poverty during the Depression years. In World War II she reported on conditions in the troops and on the home front. She worked to improve hospitals for the mentally ill and equal rights and better working conditions for women. Following her husband's death she was appointed a delegate to the United Nations and as chairperson of the Commission on Human Rights, helped to write the Universal Declaration of Human Rights.

Mary A. Hallaren 1907 -

Little did Mary Hallaren know that her life as a school teacher and world traveler would drastically change with the beginning of World War II. Before that time she had done walking tours of most of the world including the Far East and South America. At the beginning of the War, the Women's Auxiliary Corps needed officers, and Mary was one of the first to be chosen for Officers Candidate School.

Her army career saw her promoted to Commanding Officer of the 1st WAAC Separate Battalion that she led in the European Theater of Operations. In 1947 she became the third Director of the Women's Army Corps. Her awards include the Legion of Merit, the Bronze Star Army Commendation Medal, and the French Legion of Honor. She retired in 1960 but continued to lecture at universities and travel the world. Because of her four-foot ten-inch height she was often referred to as "The Little Colonel," much admired for her championship for opportunities for military women.

Elizabeth (Betty) Robinson Schwartz 1911 - 1999

Betty Robinson was a tomboy who showed exceptional talent for running. In 1928 this talent earned her a place on the United States Olympic track team. The choice was a good one as she brought honor to the nation by winning a gold medal.

In 1931 her track career came to a halt. She was badly injured in a plane crash, and her recovery was painful and slow. Betty was determined, however, to gain back the skills she had lost and fought for four years to bring her broken body back to peak performance. Her amazing recovery led her to once again be a member of the United States Olympic track team where she and her team members in the relay race came home with another gold!

Mary Martin 1913 - 1990

Mary Martin was born to dance. As a child she performed at every opportunity, including a local fireman's dinner where she saw the fire pole and dreamed of sliding down. As a young woman with no formal training in dance she opened her own dance studio in Dallas, Texas. She took lessons in nearby Fort Worth, then taught her students what she had been taught.

When her studio burned to the ground, she went to Hollywood as one of many young hopefuls. Getting noticed by studio heads was nearly impossible until the night she performed an original routine at a local club and was spotted as star quality. She starred in many movies, but her greatest success was on Broadway in the role of Peter Pan where she made sure she would slide down a fire pole! Her son, Larry Hagman also became a star, best known for his role in the hit TV series *Dallas*.

Frances Oldham Kelsey 1914 -

From childhood Frances Oldham dreamed of being a scientist. She achieved her dream by graduating from McGill University in Canada and earning her doctorate at the University of Chicago. She undertook research studies on the effect of drugs on the body with Dr. Fremont Kelsey whom she married in 1943. Their studies were the first to show the effect of drugs on developing embryos. Frances Kelsey earned a medical degree while having two children during the four-year course of study. She accepted a job with the Food and Drug Administration to evaluate applications from drug companies to market new drugs. One of these drugs was Thalidomide, a sleeping pill used by thousands in Europe and thought to be safe. The pressure on Dr. Kelsey to approve the drug was tremendous. However, she felt they needed more information and delayed her decision again and again. The drug, which was never approved for use in the United States, proved to be one that caused severe birth defects. Despite the tremendous pressures to approve the drug, Dr. Kelsey's refusal saved the lives of 1000s of unborn American children.

Mary Kay Ash d. 2001

While Mary Kay's birth date has always been kept a secret, she learned responsibility at a young age. While her mother worked long hours in a restaurant, Mary Kay took care of her invalid father as well as doing all of the cooking and cleaning. After high school she began a career in sales with Stanley Home Products. A failed marriage left her the sole support of her children. She then became the national training director for the World Gift Company. Even though she excelled at the job and became a member of the Board of Directors, they promoted a man she had trained over her. She left the company, took all the money she had, and started her own company to sell a skin softener. By her second year in business she had close to one million dollars in sales. Her "You can do it" philosophy plus a willingness to work hard, that she passed on to her growing sales force of housewives, was the secret to her success.

Delores Fernandez Huerta 1930-

A child of divorced parents, Delores Fernandez knew tough times. She did well in her studies and earned a college degree. Delores decided to devote her life to bettering the lot of Hispanic laborers, especially migrant workers. She spoke out about the harsh living conditions, poor wages and mistreatment of migrants. She helped to found the National Farm Workers Association and was instrumental in lobbying the California Legislature to pass the first bill of rights for farm workers. She taught citizenship classes, encouraged workers to vote, led boycotts and raised funds. In 1988 she was beaten in a demonstration and severely injured. But as soon as she recovered, she continued her fight on behalf of the workers.

Mary Lou Retton 1968 -

In 1984 Mary Lou Retton became the star of the Olympics by winning five medals. The most prestigious of these was the all-around in which she received the gold medal for scoring perfect 10s in gymnastics. Six weeks before the Los Angeles competition, Mary Lou broke a cartilage in her knee and the doctors who performed the surgery told her she would have to take herself out of the competition. Hard work to rehabilitate the knee paid off and resulted in the gold medal.

Mary Ellen Weber 1962 -

Mary Ellen holds degrees in chemical engineering and physical chemistry and is an avid skydiver, receiving a silver medal in the U.S. Skydiving Championships. She is a pilot whom NASA selected in 1992 to be one of fourteen astronauts to take part in the construction of the International Space Station, flying a 60-foot robotic arm and directing the transfer of thousands of pounds of equipment, logging more than 450 hours in space.

INDEX